Jenny Mosley's

TOP 100

Playground Games

to Enjoy SEAL Outside

Acknowledgements

I love games, although I'm very slow at learning them. I put this down to being left-handed as a child at a time when many teachers insisted that children should be right-handed. Hence, I now panic about any organised game with rules, which means that while I can conceptualise and research games, I get 'silly' when trying them out. However, children are my greatest teachers in this regard. They grasp ideas quickly and are endlessly patient and non-judgemental. In Corsham Regis Primary School, one of the schools I'm currently working in, we have just started a system whereby the children have the responsibility of teaching playground games. Successful children get a good teacher sticker/token, and the child/children who have learned the game get a good learner one. I should like to thank all the bright wonderful children who have shared their ideas for games with me.

I should also like to thank Corin Redsell, LDA's editorial manager, for supporting my passion for playgrounds. He is always open to new ideas or to revitalising older ones, and always tries to find a way of getting them into a busy publishing schedule. Thank you, Corin, for being patient and supportive, and for upholding the golden rules of kindness and gentleness.

Permission to photocopy

This book contains materials which may be reproduced by photocopier or other means for use by the purchaser. The permission is granted on the understanding that these copies will be used within the educational establishment of the purchaser. The book and all its contents remain copyright. Copies may be made without reference to the publisher or the licensing scheme for the making of photocopies operated by the Publishers' Licensing Agency.

The right of Jenny Mosley to be identified as the author of this work has been asserted by her in accordance with sections 77 and 78 of the Copyright, Designs and Patents Act 1988.

Jenny Mosley's Top 100 Playground Games to Enjoy SEAL Outside
100772
ISBN-13: 978 1 85503 473 0

© Jenny Mosley
All rights reserved
First published 2008
Reprinted 2009

Printed in the UK for LDA
Pintail Close, Victoria Business Park, Nottingham, NG4 2SG

Contents

Introduction 7

Motivation

Foot out, hand in 9
The big fish 10
Eye can see you 11
Court 12
What's the time, Mr Wolf? 13
Bing bong 14
Triangular teamball 15
Mirror walk 16
Frogs 17
Spies 18
Not me, sir. Him, sir 19
Beat the box 20
Slick squares 21
Stuck in the middle 22
Lucky 13 23
Quick mimes 24
Tip and run 25
Feetball 26
Gemini tag 27
At the bottom of the sea 28

Social skills

Who stole the cookies from the cookie jar? 29
I like you because 30
Squeaking mice 31
Blowing balloons 32
The ogre's castle 33
Rabbit in the warren 34
Crocodile shock 35
Wordball 36
Roll, roll, roll the ball 37
Colourful conversations 38
Flip a coin 39
Bear trap 40

Contents

Simon says it twice 41

Percussion band 42

Matching pairs 43

Airborne 44

Running pairs 45

Circling round 46

Back pass 47

Noisy beanbags 48

Hang on to it 49

Shoulders back 50

Zoo 51

Sheep, sheep, come home 52

Rainmaker 53

Bingo 54

Pop idol 55

The nickname game 56

The troll's road 57

Finding a home 58

The interceptor 59

Exaggeration 60

Humming bees 61

Managing feelings

Secret signs 62

Human paper, scissors, stone 63

Over and under 64

Noughts and crosses 65

Every letter 66

Master of the Nile 67

Cat and mouse 68

Not today, thank you 69

Beat the bounce 70

French cricket 71

Box the beanbag 72

I had a little puppy 73

Empathy

Numbers 74
Going fishing 75
Sharks and fishes 76
How are you? 77
Eggs in the nest 78
Wandering tribes 79
Rag tag 80
Come up smiling 81
Changing feelings 82
The same game 83
Put up, put down 84
Birthdays 85
Show some emotion 86
Shaping feelings 87
Mirror 88
You know me 89
Cops and robbers 90
Building blocks 91

Self-awareness

Hot potato 92
North, south, east and west 93
Colour catch 94
The trickster's choice 95
The magic finger 96
Jumbled jobs 97
Fizz buzz 98
Pass the invisible object 99
Green light, red light 100
I'm happy 101
Band, book or beast 102
Chinese whispers 103
Popping corn 104
It's the way that you do it 105
Caterpillar 106
Fortunately, unfortunately 107
Two little dicky-birds 108

Training
109

Books and resources
110

Introduction

In the past, children passed their lore and culture down the generations as they played together outside. This play would have included rhymes and riddles, rituals and rites of passage, and, importantly, a wealth of games that didn't require adult supervision. In time, these games became part of school playtimes, and were an ideal way to learn social skills and generate a sense of community.

Today, children have fewer opportunities to teach each other in this rewarding way and often need support to get them started. This book is intended to help you to get the ball rolling in your setting. It includes some original games and a range of traditional ones that have been revitalised. As well as being a lot of fun, these games will also allow teachers and lunchtime supervisors to help children to benefit from the social and emotional skills that each game involves.

Careful planning and organisation should mean that you only need to teach a game once. In time, the children will make it their own and share it with each year's new intake, who will continue this process, ensuring that a tradition of playing games will be established in your setting, benefiting the whole school community.

You might decide, as many schools are, to give this book to some of your children straight away, so they can be the first ones to get your playground games initiative going.

The games are presented under the following headings:

- **O** Motivation
- **O** Social skills
- **O** Managing feelings
- **O** Empathy
- **O** Self-awareness.

These relate to the skills mentioned in the government's social and emotional aspects of learning (SEAL) materials of 2005. Each game's focus is informed by the statements from Appendix 1 of the SEAL guidance booklet. This means that when you are focusing on a particular skill as part of your curriculum, you can select and teach the games that will reinforce what is happening in your classroom.

If used in this way, playground games become more than simply a source of pleasure and excitement as they have the added benefit of taking something from the classroom into the wider world of children's lives.

We have made every effort to provide games that require little or no equipment. Any equipment that is needed should be readily available in your setting. All of the games are designed to be enjoyable and fun, and many are non-competitive. With such a wealth of games included, we hope you will select those that tie in with your curriculum needs and reflect the ethos of your setting.

We have created new games and updated many others to make them accessible. However, we feel strongly that, if playground games are to survive, children need to be taught them and then encouraged to take imaginative ownership of them, adapting them to their own use. So, with the help of some willing adults, teach children some new games regularly and look forward to seeing your efforts bear fruit. Enjoy seeing the games change as the children you work with enhance them and make them an exhilarating part of the vibrant culture of your school community.

Foot out, hand in

SEAL skill

We know how to direct our attention and concentrate on things of importance.

Resources

Plastic hoops or playground chalk

What to do

Place the hoops at various points at least 5 metres apart on the playing area. Use the chalk to draw circles if you don't have any hoops. The hoops are safe zones.

Choose two children to be catchers. Ask the other children to stand so that they have one foot outside of a hoop and one hand touching the ground inside the same hoop. If a child loses their balance, they must run to another hoop. At that point, the catchers must try to apprehend them by touching them on the shoulder.

If a child gets safely to another hoop, they stand as before. If they are caught, they must go to the edge of the playing area and do ten star jumps before rejoining the game.

Swap the catchers regularly.

Comments

Other exercises and penalties may be given to the children who are caught.

Vary the distance between the hoops depending on the age of the children.

The big fish

SEAL skill

We know how to keep trying when things get difficult.

Resources

None

What to do

Ask the children to form a circle. Choose one child to be the angler and ask them to stand out of sight of the group briefly. Choose a second child, ask them to walk round the outside of the circle and tap one of the children on their back before finding a place in the circle. They must do this without the other children spotting who they have chosen. The nominated child is the big fish, while the other children are standard fish.

Ask the angler to stand in the centre of the circle. Explain that the big fish is going to try to kill off other fish in the circle by pouting at them. If the big fish pouts at one of the fish, they must flap their hands like fins before falling to the ground. The angler must try to work out who the big fish is. Allow them three guesses. If they are successful, choose a new angler. If they fail, play another round with the same angler.

Comments

Instead of a fish, use a frog that sticks out its tongue, a murderer who winks or a bandit who mimes using a gun made with the finger and thumb of one of their hands.

Eye can see you

SEAL skill

We can choose to direct our attention, concentrate and resist distractions for increasing periods of time.

Resources

None

What to do

Ask the children to stand in a circle and choose a child (Child A) to stand in the centre of it. They move around in the circle, looking at each child in turn. At some point, they must wink at a child (Child B). The game then proceeds in the following way:

- Child B winks at someone across the circle (Child C).
- Child C runs round the outside of the circle before taking Child B's place.
- Child B replaces Child A.
- Child A takes Child C's place.

A new round begins.

Comments

Play as above, but tell Child A to call 'Time' after a period of their choosing, at which point those children who winked at someone point at the relevant person. Child A chooses a child who is not pointing to be the new Child A. If everyone is pointing, allow Child A an unrestricted choice.

Court

SEAL skill

We can stay focused even when under pressure.

Resources

None

What to do

Ask the children to sit in a circle, choose a child to be the lawyer and ask them to stand in the centre of the circle. They must approach a child and say, 'Starting from now, you must not say a word when I speak to you. You must not nod, smile or respond in any other way.'

The lawyer is allowed to ask the child three questions on any subject in an attempt to elicit a response from them. If the child does respond, they are out of the game and the lawyer moves on to another child. However, if the lawyer fails to catch a child out, this child becomes the new lawyer and the previous lawyer takes their place in the circle. A new round begins with everyone participating.

Comments

Try using a clown instead of a lawyer. Their task is to try to eliminate children by making them laugh. Alternatively, use a chef. A child is out if they respond to the chef's descriptions of their wonderful meals.

What's the time, Mr Wolf?

SEAL skill

We can set a challenge and consider the consequences.

Resources

None

What to do

Choose someone to be Mr Wolf and ask them to stand at the end of the playground with their back to everybody. The other players stand on a line at the other end of the playground facing Mr Wolf. The game proceeds as follows:

○ The players chant: *What's the time, Mr Wolf?*

○ Without looking back, Mr Wolf says a time; for example: *Five o'clock.*

○ The players then take five steps forward and repeat their question.

○ Mr Wolf says another time, which the players respond to.

○ This continues until Mr Wolf says: *Dinner time.*

○ Mr Wolf then chases everyone back home, trying to catch one of them.

○ The player who is caught becomes the new Mr Wolf in the next game.

○ If Mr Wolf doesn't catch anyone, they have to be Mr Wolf again.

If a player reaches Mr Wolf before dinner time, they tap Mr Wolf on the shoulder and run for home. Mr Wolf tries to catch a player in the same way as before.

Comments

Use a dragon that says 'Fire-breathing time' or an ogre that says 'Bone-crunching time'.

Bing bong

SEAL skill

We can overcome frustration.

Resources

Two sticks or other small objects

What to do

Ask the children to sit or stand in a circle. Give the objects to one child (Child A). The game proceeds as follows:

- Child A passes one object to the child on their right (Child B), saying: *This is a bing.*

- Child B says: *A what?*

- Child A repeats: *A bing.*

- Child B says: *Thank you.*

The object continues round the circle in this manner.

Child A passes the other object to their left saying: *This is a bong.*

They have the same dialogue about the bong before it proceeds round the circle.

The game continues with the two objects travelling in different directions round the circle as quickly as possible. Players have three lives. Each time they make a mistake, they lose a life. If a player loses all their lives, they sit with their arms folded until the game ends.

Comments

Nominate a child to be a time-keeper and keep a record of how quickly the objects are passed successfully round the circle.

Triangular teamball

SEAL skill

We can keep going even when our team is not doing well.

Resources

A large ball and three pairs of PE markers

What to do

Set up a goal using a pair of markers at each point of a large imaginary triangle. Divide the children into three teams and choose a leader for each team. Each leader goes into the triangle. Allocate each team a goal, which must be defended by the other team members.

Team leaders take it in turn to try to score a point by kicking, throwing or rolling the ball into one of the goals of their opponents. They can score directly or by passing it to a team-mate, who can then attempt to score.

The team with the highest score after an agreed period of time is the winner.

Comments

Use more than one ball to increase the difficulty of the game.

Mirror walk

SEAL skill

We can concentrate and resist distractions.

Resources

None

What to do

Divide the group into pairs. Ask each pair to decide who will be the leader and the follower in their group. The follower in each pair must stay about a metre behind their leader at all times.

The leaders may walk any where in the playground, with their followers trying to remain a metre behind them. Leaders are allowed to perform actions that the followers must copy.

When two leaders meet, each leader gives the other one of the following instructions:

- Change places – the leader becomes the follower

- No change – roles within the pair remain the same

- Swap partners – the pair splits up and each member looks for a new partner from another pair that has split up.

Comments

Vary the number of instructions the leaders may give depending on the size of the group.

Frogs

SEAL skill

We can bounce back after a disappointment.

Resources

None

What to do

Ask the children to form a circle and squat like a frog with their hands by their sides. Choose one child to be the leader and ask them to stand in the middle of the circle.

When the leader says 'In the pond', the frogs must put their hands palms downwards on the floor in front of them. When the leader says 'On the bank', the frogs must place their hands in their laps.

If the leader spots anyone who is not responding correctly, that child is out and must sit with their arms folded until the next game. The leader will need to call the instructions quickly to catch out as many frogs as possible.

Comments

Vary the animal and instructions used to keep this game fresh.

Spies

SEAL skill

We know how to stay alert.

Resources

None

What to do

Choose one child to be the mark and tell them to walk round the playing area. The remaining children are spies. Choose a child to be the spymaster from this group.

The spymaster must lead the spies as they follow the mark. However, the mark is allowed to try to capture one of the spies at any moment. When they try, the spymaster must respond quickly by shouting 'Down'. The spies must crouch at this signal. The mark cannot tag a spy who is crouching.

Any spy caught by the mark is out of the game until all the spies are caught or the mark calls 'All change', at which point a different mark is chosen and a new game begins.

Comments

The mark could be a fox, with the spymaster as a mother duck and the other children as her ducklings.

Not me, sir. Him, sir

SEAL skill

We know how to maintain our concentration.

Resources

None

What to do

Ask the children to stand in a circle. Choose a child to be the leader and ask them to stand in the centre of the circle.

The leader looks round the circle sternly and says, 'Joey's lost his marbles and I think I know who's got them.' They point at a child and say 'It's you.'

The nominated child must point quickly at another child and say, 'Not me, sir. Him/Her, sir.' Any child who hesitates or shows any emotion is out of the game and must stand with their arms folded. The game continues until one child is left, who becomes the new leader.

Comments

If the leader points at someone who is already out, a new leader is chosen.

Beat the box

SEAL skill

We know that enthusiasm will help us to succeed.

Resources

A box of balls

What to do

Choose a child to be the thrower and ask the other children to stand a short distance away from them.

The thrower takes a ball from the box and throws it as far as they can in any direction. They do the same with the other balls. While this is happening, the other children must try to return the balls to the box as quickly as possible, so that the thrower doesn't empty it.

If the thrower does empty the box, they win. If the thrower becomes tired, they may call 'Time', in which case all the balls are returned to the box and a new thrower is chosen.

Comments

You might want to use more than one thrower if you have a large group.

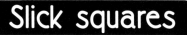
Slick squares

SEAL skill

We know how to cope with disappointment.

Resources

A ball for each team

What to do

Divide the children into groups of four, asking each team to form a large square with a 4-metre space between each group member. Number the children in each team beginning at one. Give Child 1 in each team a ball.

At your signal, Child 1 must throw the ball to Child 2 in their square, who throws it to Child 3, and so on round the square back to Child 1. The first team to complete seven such circuits is the winner. However, if a player drops the ball, their team's number of circuits is cancelled and they must start again.

Comments

Adjust the number of circuits depending on the age and ability of the children.

Stuck in the middle

SEAL skill

We know how to stay calm despite feelings of irritation.

Resources

A soft ball

What to do

Ask the children to stand in a well-spaced circle. Choose three children to stand in the centre of the circle. Give the ball to one of the other children.

The child with the ball starts the game by throwing it using both hands at the children in the centre. If they hit one of them below the knee then that child is out and steps out of the circle. If they miss, the child who catches the ball has a throw, and so on.

Once all the children are out, choose three new children to go into the circle.

Comments

Use more than one ball if your group is proficient at this game.

Lucky 13

SEAL skill

We know how to think before we act.

Resources

None

What to do

Put the children into groups of four and ask each group to form a square. Tell the children to put their hands behind their back.

Explain that at your command each team member must choose a number and place their hand(s) in the centre of the square with that number of digits showing, with a fist counting as zero. The aim is to have thirteen digits showing in total. The team nearest 13 scores a point. If there is more than one team that is the closest, they both receive a point. No discussion is allowed in this game.

Continue playing until one team has scored five points.

Comments

If a team's total in one round is 13, they receive two points.

Quick mimes

SEAL skill

We know how to stay focused.

Resources

None

What to do

Ask the children to stand in a circle and choose a child to lead the game. Ask this child to perform a simple mime of their choosing – brushing their hair, cleaning their teeth, and so on. Everyone in the circle must copy this mime.

The leader must point to another child at a time of their choosing, but try to keep the game pacy. This child must change the mime to a new one, which the group must copy. Any child who you feel reacted too slowly to a change must count to ten before rejoining the game.

Comments

You might like to play the game using speech instead of actions, with children using nursery rhymes or well-known songs.

Tip and run

SEAL skill

We know how to deal with disappointment and can bounce back when things don't go as planned.

Resources

A softball or rounders bat and ball, and two PE markers

What to do

Choose a child to be the batter. Ask them to stand beside one of the markers. Place the other marker 3 metres to the left of the batter. Choose a second child to be the bowler. Ask them to stand an appropriate distance from the batter, depending on the age of the children involved. Give the bat to the batter and the ball to the bowler. The remaining children are the fielders and must find a place to stand in the playing area.

Play begins with the bowler bowling the ball to the batter. If the batter hits the ball, they must run round the marker to their left and back again. This counts as one run.

If a fielder catches the ball hit by the batter before it bounces, the batter is out and the fielder replaces them. A fielder or bowler may run out a batter by hitting the marker the batter is approaching with the ball. A player who achieves this becomes the new batter.

The child who scores the most runs is the winner.

Comments

Use different PE equipment to develop other skills – a football, tennis-racket and ball, and so on.

Feetball

SEAL skill

We can bounce back when things go wrong.

Resources

A small ball and a PE marker for each team

What to do

Divide the children into small teams of equal number. Ask the teams to go to an agreed line across one end of the playing area and each form a line facing along the playing area. Place a marker about 3 metres in front of each team.

Give the first child in each line a ball. At your command, they must grip their ball between their feet and jump to their marker and back. They then hand the ball to the next person in their team who does the same, and so on.

If a player loses control of their ball on the way to their marker, they must begin their go again. However, if the ball is dropped on the way back, they must collect it and resume their go from the point at which they lost the ball.

The team that finishes first is the winner.

Comments

Try carrying the ball using other body parts – beneath the chin, held under an arm, between the knees, and so on.

Gemini tag

SEAL skill

We can choose where to direct our attention in order to succeed.

Resources

None

What to do

Choose one child to be the chaser. Ask the other children to form pairs, linking arms with their partner. The pairs then spread out in the playing area.

When the game begins, the chaser must try to tag a pair. Pairs try to avoid being tagged by running away from the chaser. If the chaser tags a pair, they separate and each one becomes a chaser.

The game ends when there are no more pairs left to tag.

Comments

Vary the way in which players are allowed to move, try heel-to-toe steps, hopping, and so on.

At the bottom of the sea

SEAL skill

We know how to practise until we can do things proficiently.

Resources

None

What to do

Teach the children the following action song. Once familiar, ask a child to lead the song.

At the bottom of the sea, (Crouch down and touch the floor)

So blue and green, (Slap thighs and clap hands x 2)

Is the biggest, fattest whale (Stretch arms up high and out wide)

You have ever seen. (Slap thighs and clap hands x 2)

He opens his mouth wide (Use arms to mime a large mouth opening)

From nose to chin, (Point to nose and chin)

And all the little silver fish (Slap thighs and clap hands x 2)

Swim right in. (Wiggle fingers)

Comments

Hold a competition to see which child can perform the song the quickest.

Who stole the cookies from the cookie jar?

SEAL skill

We can work well in a group and cooperate with others.

Resources

None

What to do

Teach the children the words to this game. Ask the children to form a circle and choose a child to lead the game. Everybody claps their hands and chants: *Who stole the cookies from the cookie jar?*

The leader calls out another child's name, for example: *Sarah.*

Everybody claps and chants: *Sarah stole the cookies from the cookie jar.*

Sarah claps and chants: *Who, me?*

Everybody claps and says: *Yes, you.*

Sarah claps and says: *Couldn't be.*

Everybody claps and says: *Then who?*

Sarah claps and calls out another name from the group, for example: *Joel.*

Everybody claps and chants: *Joel stole the cookies from the cookie jar.*

The game continues as before.

Comments

Use different foods and receptacles – fruit and fruit bowl, pizza and pizza box, and so on.

I like you because ...

SEAL skill

We recognise put-downs and know that they affect people, so we try not to use them.

Resources

None

What to do

Ask the children to form a circle and choose a child to lead the game. The leader walks round the outside of the circle. At some point, they must tap a child on the shoulder. This child must close their eyes.

The leader says 'Hum', at which point everyone in the group must hum quietly. While they are humming, the leader whispers the name of another child in the group in the tapped child's ear. The tapped child must keep their eyes closed and describe the named player, exploring their appearance, personality, strengths and preferences. All observations must be positive. The tapped child must also say one thing they like about the child.

The other players must raise their hand when they think they know who is being described. When the tapped child opens their eyes, they must ask volunteers for their suggestions. If a volunteer identifies the child, they become the new leader and a new round begins. If they guess incorrectly, the tapped child is allowed to choose another volunteer, and so on until someone guesses correctly.

Comments

You may choose other things for the tapped children to describe, such as types of weather, different sports, and so on.

Squeaking mice

SEAL skill

We can work well with others.

Resources

None

What to do

Ask the children to form a long curved line. Choose one child to be the cat. The other children are the mice. Ask the cat to stand a short distance away with their back to the mice.

The mice need to form a huddle and quietly choose one child to be the squeaker. The mice then re-form the line.

Ask the cat to face the mice. The squeaker must try to squeak regularly without being spotted by the cat. If the cat guesses who the squeaker is, they must explain how they managed it before having another go. If they are unsuccessful, the squeaker reveals themselves and explains their winning tactics. The squeaker swaps with the cat and a new round begins.

Comments

Use different themes to keep the game fresh. Try using a car that makes a beeping sound that needs to be spotted by a police officer, or a chicken that makes a clucking noise that must be spotted by a fox.

Blowing balloons

SEAL skill

We can cooperate with others to achieve a joint outcome.

Resources

None

What to do

Ask the children to form a circle and choose one child to be the blower. The blower stands in the centre of the circle. Those remaining in the circle hold hands and form a tight circle.

The blower pretends to blow up a balloon. As they do so, the children in the circle begin to walk backwards slowly making the circle bigger. When the circle reaches the point at which its members can't hold hands any longer, the balloon 'bursts' and the children spin away.

Comments

Choose a child to be the winder. They must mime pulling a rope, causing a big circle to decrease in size. When the winder says 'Wind it down', the circle must expand again.

The ogre's castle

SEAL skill

We know how to involve everyone in the fun.

Resources

None

What to do

Choose a child to be the ogre and ask them to stand in the middle of the playing area. Divide the remaining children into two groups – Team 1 and Team 2. Ask each team to stand at opposite ends of the playing area.

When the ogre shouts 'One' or 'Two', the children in the relevant team must attempt to run to the opposite end of the playing area. If the ogre touches a child on the shoulder, they must stand still. When all the children from the named team have finished their crossing or been tagged, the other team attempts to cross. As they cross, they must try to release any of the tagged children by touching them on the shoulder. If they release someone without being tagged themselves, the released child stands at the side of the playing area, while the other child continues to the other end. The released child takes no further part in the game.

Play continues in this way until only one child is free, who becomes the new ogre, or an agreed amount of time has passed.

Comments

Use two ogres if you have a large number of players.

Rabbit in the warren

SEAL skill

We know how to join in with a large group.

Resources

None

What to do

This is a game played in groups of fifteen children. In each group, choose one child to be the fox, another to be the rabbit and a third to be the farmer. The remaining twelve children form a grid of four rows of three. Each child in the grid must hold hands with the child/children next to them in their row. These rows represent the walls of the rabbit warren.

Ask the rabbit to choose a place to start in the warren. Tell the fox to take up a position a row away from the rabbit. The farmer must stand next to you. On your command, the fox must chase the rabbit and try to catch it. If the farmer shouts 'Turn', the fox and rabbit must stand still while the children in the grid let go of the hand(s) they are holding and turn 90 degrees to form three columns of four children holding hands. The chase can then resume.

When the rabbit has been caught or an agreed amount of time has passed, choose a new rabbit, fox and farmer and play a new game.

Comments

Fair play is important in this game to ensure that no-one is injured.

Crocodile shock

SEAL skill

We can play together so that each of us feels happy.

Resources

None

What to do

Ask the children to stand in a circle and choose one child to be the hunter. The hunter must walk round the outside of the circle. As they do so, they must gently draw a wiggly line down the back of each child that they pass, saying 'Snake, snake' as they do so. A touched child must respond by hissing.

At any time the hunter may touch either side of a child's waist and say 'Crocodile'. If this happens, the crocodile must chase the hunter round the outside of the circle. While this is happening, the other children clap their hands to simulate the crocodile's snapping jaws. If the crocodile catches the hunter, they become the new hunter. However, if the hunter reaches the vacated space in the circle, they continue in their role.

Comments

Choose different themes for the game. If you use cars, ask a child to be a mechanic, rather than a hunter. They name each child an old banger, which the children respond to by making a groaning noise. 'Crocodile' may be replaced by 'Ferrari'.

Wordball

SEAL skill

We can resolve conflicts and adhere to others' judgements.

Resources

A soft ball

What to do

Ask the children to stand in a circle. Choose one child to begin the game and give them the ball. Choose two other children to be judges and ask them to stand outside of the circle.

The child with the ball begins the game by throwing it to someone else. As they throw the ball, they say a word loudly and clearly. The child who catches the ball must quickly say a related word. The judges must decide if the word given relates to the thrower's word. If they think it does, the game continues. If they don't think it does, the child who gave the word has an opportunity to explain the reasons for their choice. If the judges are convinced by the reasons given, the game continues. If they aren't, the child who gave the word sits out of the game. The game continues until only two players are left.

Comments

Vary the criterion for the choosing of words, try using words that must rhyme, or a theme with limited options, such as colours, meaning that repetition must be avoided.

Roll, roll, roll the ball

SEAL skill

We know how to be friendly and treat each other with respect.

Resources

A soft ball

What to do

Ask the children to stand in a circle and give one child the ball. They start the game by calling out the name of someone else in the circle and rolling the ball to them. The named child says 'Thank you' when they receive the ball, to which the sender replies 'You're welcome.' The ball is then passed to another player and the game continues.

Comments

Vary the dialogue used, such as 'Good Morning, [Child's name]. How are you today?' The reply being 'I'm fine, thank you.'

Colourful conversations

SEAL skill

We know how to make friendships.

Resources

Three beanbags of the same colour per group – try to have as wide a range of colours as possible

What to do

Put the children into groups of three and give each group three beanbags of the same colour. Explain that the purpose of the game is to collect three beanbags each of a different colour. This is done by exchanging a beanbag with someone in a different group. In order to exchange beanbags, each child must find something out about the child they intend to swap with. The first group to achieve this is the winner.

When the first group has finished, call all the groups to you and allow each group in turn to share the information they found out from the other groups.

Comments

You may use cards or balls of different colours if you prefer.

The children may use notepads and pencils to write down the information they receive.

Flip a coin

SEAL skill

We can play with other children in a way that ensures that everyone feels that the game is fair and safe.

Resources

A coin

What to do

Ask the children to form a large circle and choose one child to be the leader. Ask them to stand in the centre of the circle holding the coin. The leader flips the coin. If the coin shows a head when it lands, the players in the circle must move in any direction using a two-footed jump. If the coin shows tails, the leader may move one pace in any direction. All players must remain still between flips of the coin.

The aim of the game for the leader is to get close enough to another player so that they can touch them on the shoulder, while keeping at least one foot on the ground. If someone is touched, they become the new leader and the game begins again.

Comments

Any object with two distinct sides may be used instead of a coin.

Having two leaders, each with their own coin, results in a faster game.

Bear trap

SEAL skill

We can have fun and remain gentle.

Resources

None

What to do

Choose four children and ask them to stand facing each other in a small circle. They need to hold hands and raise their arms above their heads to make the bear trap. Choose another child to be the trapper. They must stand with their back to the bear trap. The remaining children are bears.

The bears must run in and out of the bear trap. When the trapper says 'Catch', the four children that make the trap lower their arms quickly. If a bear is caught in the trap, they become part of the trap, which grows in size. When four free bears are left, they create a bear trap and a new game begins.

Comments

The trap could be for another animal such as a mouse. The trapper would then say 'Cheese' instead of 'Catch'.

Simon says it twice

SEAL skill

We know how to work well as part of a group.

Resources

None

What to do

Divide the children into two groups and ask each group to choose someone to be Simon. When the game begins, each Simon gives instructions to their group in the traditional manner. If they begin an instruction with 'Simon says', then the group must respond. If an instruction is given without these words, then the group must not respond. If a child responds inappropriately, they are out of their group's game. However, they may run to the other group and join in their game.

Comments

Change the instructions round to vary the game so that the children must remember not to do what Simon says.

Percussion band

SEAL skill

We can take instructions respectfully from our peers.

Resources

Simple untuned percussion instruments

What to do

The children will need to use untuned percussion instruments or parts of their body to make a range of sounds. Ask each musician in turn to demonstrate the sound they will be making to the group, then appoint a band leader.

The band leader must organise the musicians into a curved line. When ready, they need to conduct the musicians to help them to produce a musical composition. This can be done by pointing to an individual who must produce a rhythmic piece using their sound, or by pointing to several children in quick succession so that the piece has more than one part.

Comments

Use a well-known song for the composition with the band playing the rhythm.

Add a choir and/or dancers to make a performance even more exciting.

Matching pairs

SEAL skill

We know how to play independently and together.

Resources

A range of playground play equipment

What to do

Give each child in the group a piece of playground play equipment, making sure that two pieces of each type of equipment are represented in the group. Tell the children that you will give them a few minutes to think about what games might be played with their piece of equipment. Once the time has elapsed, ask them to find a partner who has the same piece of equipment as them. Each pair must work together to devise a game using their equipment. After 10 minutes, ask the pairs to join you and ask each in turn to demonstrate their game.

Comments

Vary the size of the groups for a different dynamic.

Allow children with different pieces of equipment to form pairs, as long as they pair up with someone they don't normally play with.

Airborne

SEAL skill

We can take turns.

Resources

A lightweight ball for each team

What to do

Divide the children into teams of equal number. Ask each team to number their members, starting from one. Give Child 1 in each group a ball.

At your command, Child 1 in each team hits the ball into the air. Child 2 in each team tries to hit the ball before it touches the ground. Team members continue this in numerical order, with Child 1 continuing the sequence once the highest number is reached. If a team's ball touches the ground, that team is out of the game. When one team is left, declare it the winner.

Comments

The game may be played without numbering team members, enabling anyone in the team to try to keep the ball in the air.

Running pairs

SEAL skill

We can cooperate even when excited.

Resources

None

What to do

Divide the children into pairs. Ask them to remain in their pairs and form a circle. Partners should hold hands. Choose one pair to be the runners. They walk round the outside of the circle and, at a time of their choosing, touch the joined hands of another pair. The runners then run anti-clockwise round the circle, while the chosen pair runs clockwise. The first pair to get back to the vacated space wins. The losing children become the runners for the next game.

Comments

Vary the way that pairs are permitted to travel round the circle – hopping, skipping, two-footed jumps, and so on.

Circling round

SEAL skill

We know that winning with grace is what winning is about.

Resources

Two balls, each a different colour

What to do

Ask the children to stand in a circle and give one of the balls to a child. Give the other ball to the child on their left. The child given the first ball names the colour of their ball. The child given the second ball does the same. The remaining children in the circle continue this alternating naming sequence in a clockwise fashion until every child has one of the two colour names.

On your command, the two children holding the balls each throw or pass their ball to their nearest team member going clockwise round the circle. The balls continue round the circle in this manner, with the winning team being the one whose ball completes the circuit the quickest. This team scores a point and the game starts again. The first team to score 10 points is the winner. Points may be deducted from a team if one of its members interferes with the other team's ball.

Comments

Differentiate between teams by giving members of a team the same colour of band to wear.

Back pass

SEAL skill

We know how to use our looking skills and still, perhaps, lose gracefully.

Resources

A small, soft ball

What to do

Ask the children to stand in a circle with their hands behind their back. Choose one child to stand in the centre of the circle. They must cover their eyes.

Give the ball to another child, who walks round the outside of the circle and quietly places the ball in someone's hands. They rejoin the circle and tell the child in the centre to uncover their eyes. The child in the centre must try to work out who has the ball. They are allowed up to three guesses. At the same time, the children in the circle must try to pass the ball round the group without being spotted.

If the child in the centre of the circle guesses correctly, they swap places with the child who had the ball. If they guess incorrectly, the game resumes and they must try again. If they use up all three of their guesses without being successful, they choose a new guesser and swap places with them.

Comments

Try using a small bell or bunch of keys instead of a ball.

Noisy beanbags

SEAL skill

We can cooperate to achieve a joint outcome.

Resources

A large number of beanbags

What to do

Distribute the beanbags on the playground. Put the children into two teams and ask each team to choose a leader. Name each team after an animal, vehicle or musical instrument that has a distinctive sound that can be replicated vocally.

Each team must try to find more beanbags than the other team. Teams may split up and search for beanbags. However, only the team leader is allowed to touch them. If a team member finds a beanbag, they must stand by it and make their team's noise in order to attract their team leader. If a team member is standing by a beanbag making their sound, another team cannot take the beanbag.

The team with the most beanbags at the end of the game wins.

Comments

Use physical signs or gestures, rather than vocal ones, as a way for team members to attract their leader.

Hang on to it

SEAL skill

We know how to work together successfully as a team.

Resources

A ball and a set of coloured bands

What to do

Divide the children into two teams. Ask the members of one team to each wear one of the bands. Ask both teams to spread out in the playing area.

Choose one child from each team to stand facing you with a small gap between them. Throw the ball high in the air. The team of whichever of the two children catches the ball starts the game. This child throws the ball to a member of their team and shouts 'One'. The catcher throws it to another member of their team and shouts 'Two'. This continues until someone from the opposing team intercepts the ball. The team that intercepted the ball then tries to build up their own sequence of catches. A player is not allowed to move while they are holding the ball.

The team with the longest sequence of catches at the end of the game is the winner.

Comments

Appoint a counter for each team if it is hard to keep track of the number of catches in a sequence.

Shoulders back

SEAL skill

We know how to be good sports when the outcome of a game doesn't go in our favour.

Resources

A soft ball

What to do

Choose a child to stand at one end of the playground with their back to the other children, who must find a space to stand in the playing area. Give the chosen child the ball. When they are ready, they throw the ball over their shoulder. The other players try to catch it. When a child has gathered the ball, all players must stand still with their hands behind their backs. They then say, '[Chosen child's name], we're ready.' The chosen child turns round and tries to guess which child is holding the ball. If they guess correctly, they swap places with the child holding the ball. If they guess incorrectly, they remain as the chosen child for another game.

Comments

Vary the rule regarding the outcome of a guess – if the chosen child guesses incorrectly, they swap with the named child. If they guess correctly, they remain the chosen child.

Play the game using two balls.

Zoo

SEAL skill

We know how to make friends with people we don't know.

Resources

None

What to do

Ask the children to stand in a circle and choose one child to stand in the centre of it. This child is the leader. Choose the names of three animals found in a zoo – monkey, lion and camel. The leader must walk round the circle giving each child the name of one of the chosen animals.

The leader returns to the centre of the circle and calls out one of the animal names. The children with this name must try to cross the circle and find a vacated space. If the leader manages to fill one of the vacated spaces, the child left without a space becomes the new leader.

If a leader calls 'Time for tea', the children in the circle must form three groups based on their animal names. Each child must give themselves a name based on their animal – Mona Monkey, Matthew Monkey – and introduce themselves to the other children in their group. When the leader calls 'Tea's over', everyone returns to the circle.

Comments

Instead of using animals found in a zoo, you could use farm animals or animals from a sea-life centre.

Sheep, sheep, come home

SEAL skill

We know how to enjoy ourselves and join a large group.

Resources

None

What to do

Choose one child to be the fox and another to be the farmer. The other children in the group are sheep. Ask the sheep to stand at one end of the playground and the farmer at the other end. The fox must stand in the middle.

The farmer says, 'Sheep, sheep, come home.' The sheep must reply, 'We're afraid of the fox.' The fox then says, 'The fox has gone to Devonshire and won't be back for seven year.'

The sheep must then run to the farmer's end of the playground, while the fox tries to catch them. Any child who is caught helps the fox as a catcher. The game is over when all the sheep have been caught.

Comments

Play the game with two foxes if you have a large number of players.

Rainmaker

SEAL skill

We can work well in a group to achieve a joint outcome.

Resources

None

What to do

Ask the children to form a circle and choose one child to be the rainmaker. They stand in the centre of the circle. The rainmaker points to one child in the circle, who starts to rub their palms together to imitate the sound of the start of a rainstorm. The rainmaker points to other children in the circle, who rub their palms together too. This continues until everyone is making the sound. The rainmaker then points to the first child again, who starts to click their fingers instead of rubbing their palms together. The rainmaker selects other children to join in as before. The same pattern is repeated for the following actions: slapping hands on knees, and stamping feet.

After the stamping, the rainmaker continues the selection process, but reversing the actions as the rainstorm subsides.

Comments

Devise a sequence for other weather conditions such as a windy or sunny day.

Bingo

SEAL skill

We know how to enjoy ourselves as a supportive group.

Resources

None

What to do

Ask the children to stand in a circle and choose a child to stand in the centre of it. Everyone chants the following:

There was a farmer, who had a dog and Bingo was his name-o. B-I-N-G-O.

For each letter chanted the child in the centre points to a different child round the circle. The child pointed to when the group chants the last letter joins the child in the centre. The game continues until one child is left, who starts the next game.

Comments

If there are not many children playing this game, the child pointed to at the end of the chant may swap places with the one in the centre.

Pop idol

SEAL skill

We know how to be good listeners.

Resources

None

What to do

Choose a child to be the band leader for the group. Explain that the other band members will need to mime playing a musical instrument of their choice. They will also need to replicate the sound of their chosen instrument by using their voice, clapping their hands and/or tapping their feet. Try to encourage as many different instruments as possible within the group.

Ask the leader of the band to start humming a well-known tune of their choice. When the tune is established, the leader must point to a child in the band, who must continue the song with their instrument, using the song's rhythm or melody. The other band members remain quiet. Allow as many band members as possible the chance to perform a solo.

As a finale, allow the band to perform in unison with each member using the sounds they invented for their instrument.

Comments

Create a number of smaller bands. After some practice, ask each band in turn to perform their song to the other bands.

The nickname game

SEAL skill

We know how to give and receive compliments.

Resources

None

What to do

Ask the children to form a circle and choose a child to stand in the centre of it. They point at someone in the circle and give them a positive nickname, explaining why they chose it, for example: 'Generous Jenny – I gave you this nickname because you share a lot.'

The game continues in this way until everyone receives a name. Don't forget to ask one of the other children for a nickname for the child in the centre of the circle.

Comments

Stress that the nicknames given must be positive and accompanied by an affirmative statement.

The troll's road

SEAL skill

We can make playtimes fun by including everyone.

Resources

None

What to do

Choose a child to be the troll and ask them to stand in the middle of the playground. Ask the remaining children to stand in a line across the playground at one end of it. The object of the game for these children is to cross the playground without being caught by the troll.

The players chant, 'Troll, troll, may we use your road?' The troll chooses something that some of the players have in common and replies; for example, 'Only if you are wearing blue shoes.' Any players who fit that category are allowed to cross to the other side. The remaining players must then try to cross without being tagged by the troll.

Any player caught by the troll becomes another troll. The game continues until one player is left.

Comments

Instead of a troll, use a keeper of a boat. In this case, the children would chant: 'Keeper, keeper, may we cross your golden river in your golden boat?'

Finding a home

SEAL skill

We know how to use our looking skills.

Resources

None

What to do

Ask the children to form a circle and study the appearance of their fellow players. Ask each child to put something from their person into the centre of the circle – a shoe, hairband, jumper, and so on.

Choose a child to begin the game by picking up an item from the centre of the circle, but not their item. They then return it to who they think it belongs to, saying, 'Hello, [child's name], I think this belongs to you.' If this is the case, the child being offered the item replies, 'Thank you, I thought I'd lost it.' If it's not the case, the child replies, 'Sorry, that's not mine, you'd better keep searching.' The child offering the item then tries another child, and so on until they find the right child.

Allow each child to return an item to another child.

Comments

If a child is offered an item that doesn't belong to them, you might want to allow them to give the offering child a clue as to who might own the item.

The interceptor

SEAL skill

We can win and lose with equal grace.

Resources

A ball

What to do

Ask the children to form a circle and choose a child to be the interceptor. Ask them to stand in the centre of the circle.

Give the ball to another child. They must try to throw the ball to someone else in the circle without the interceptor catching it. The game continues until the interceptor catches the ball, or a suitable amount of time has elapsed. If the interceptor gets the ball, the child that threw it swaps places with the interceptor. If time runs out, choose a new interceptor.

Comments

Try playing the game with two balls, two interceptors or both.

Exaggeration

SEAL skill

We use our looking skills with others.

Resources

None

What to do

Divide the children into groups of four or five. Ask each group to stand in a line shoulder to shoulder. The child at the right-hand end of a line begins the game by making a small movement with a part of their body. The child on their left performs this movement making it slightly larger. This continues along the line with each child making the movement a little larger. When the movement reaches the end of the line, it needs to return, getting smaller as it goes.

Comments

Play so that each child continues to perform their movement after it has passed to the next child in their line.

Humming bees

SEAL skill

We can use our listening skills to make friends.

Resources

None

What to do

Ask the children to form a large inward-facing circle. All the children must close their eyes and raise their arms in front of them. Then they must hum like a bee and walk slowly towards the centre of the circle. If they touch someone, they stand still with their hands down and eyes open alongside the child they touched.

Any players who have not found a partner must keep humming and walking until they do. Those children who have found a partner may help to guide the humming children to each other.

Comments

Try the game using other animal sounds and related movements.

Secret signs

SEAL skill

We can work in pairs to come up with ideas.

Resources

None

What to do

Divide the children into pairs and explain that you want each pair to think of a question and answer that they can communicate using a sign language of their own devising. Allow them five minutes to do this.

When the time has elapsed, call the group together and invite each pair in turn to perform their question and answer to the group. The other children must try to work out what is being communicated between the pair. Ask for suggestions as to what was being said. Once the sign language has been interpreted, ask another pair to perform their dialogue.

Comments

It might help if the children make vocal noises, as well as using gestures.

This activity is a helpful way for children to understand some of the communication issues that face people with hearing difficulties.

Human paper, scissors, stone

SEAL skill

We understand that luck is a part of life.

Resources

None

What to do

This is a game for groups of three – two players and a starter. On the starter's word, each of the two players chooses paper, scissors or stone by adopting one of the following poses:

- Paper – standing up straight with arms stretched upwards
- Stone – arms wrapped round the body
- Scissors – arms and legs held to form a star shape.

The following rules apply:

- Paper beats stone, but not scissors.
- Stone beats scissors, but not paper.
- Scissors beat paper, but not stone.

If two of the same item are displayed, the heat is replayed.

The winner of the heat then plays the starter, and the loser becomes the starter. The champion is the first child to six wins in a group.

Comments

You might want to hold a championship, with the champion from each group competing to become the overall champion.

Over and under

SEAL skill

We can play and still create calm when needed.

Resources

Enough balls for one per team

What to do

Divide the children into three groups of equal number. Ask the groups to each form a forward-facing line. Give a ball to the child at the front of each line.

On your command, each player with a ball must pass it over their head to the child behind them. This child passes it under their legs to the next child. The ball continues down the line, with children alternating how it is passed as required. When the player at the back of a line receives a ball, they run to the front of their line and begin the sequence again.

No shouting or unsporting behaviour is allowed.

Comments

Larger or smaller balls may be used, as may other objects. Small balls may be passed from chin to chin, while larger balls may be held between the knees and passed on.

Noughts and crosses

SEAL skill

We can be leaders and followers.

Resources

A piece of chalk and two sets of coloured PE bands

What to do

You need ten children for this game. If you have more, set up more than one game.

Divide the children into two teams, giving each team a set of coloured PE bands. Name one team 'Noughts' and the other team 'Crosses'. Choose a leader for each team. Draw a large three by three grid on the playground.

Ask the leader of Noughts to place one of their group in a square on the grid. The leader of Crosses then places one of their players. This continues until one team leader has placed three of their players in a line vertically, horizontally or diagonally. This team is the winner. If all the places in the grid are filled and no team has won, declare the game void and play it again. Both teams discuss their strategy for the next game and select a new leader.

Comments

You might want to set up a knock-out tournament if you have a number of teams playing.

Every letter

SEAL skill

We can be followers and leaders.

Resources

None

What to do

Put the children into groups of three and ask each group to choose a three-letter word. Each team member must take a different letter from their word and devise a mime to illustrate it. For example, each letter of the word 'tea' might be mimed in the following way:

- o   T – a mime of someone talking
- o   E – a mime of someone eating
- o   A – a mime of someone being angry.

After some practice time, ask each team in turn to mime their letters in the order in which they appear in their word. The other groups must try to work out the letters. When all three letters have been mimed, the team that works out the word first is the winner. Ask them to comment constructively on the mimes they saw. They then mime the letters for their word.

If a team that has already mimed their word guesses the word of another group, they may choose which of the remaining teams to perform their mimes may go next.

Comments

Play the game with longer words and bigger teams, or use a word list that the groups must choose from.

Master of the Nile

SEAL skill

We can be calm if we want to.

Resources

None

What to do

Ask the children to form a circle and choose a child to be Pharaoh. Pharaoh must stand in the centre of the circle and say:

I am the pharaoh,

Your lord and master,

I ban all fun

And I ban all laughter.

If you grin or if you smile,

I will make you cross the Nile.

Pharaoh then tries to make the other children grin or smile by telling a joke, making a funny face, and so on. If they succeed, the child or children who reacted must cross the circle in the way Pharaoh commands – on hands and knees, doing a silly walk, pretending to swim through shark-infested water.

Comments

You can adapt the game and the rhyme to fit with your current topic – the pharaoh might become Henry VIII and the Nile might become the Thames, for instance.

Cat and mouse

SEAL skill

We can keep ourselves calm and quiet when necessary.

Resources

A small tin with a lid partially filled with dried beans, buttons or counters

What to do

Ask the children to form a circle and choose one child to be the cat. They crouch in the centre of the circle and cover their eyes with their hands, pretending to be asleep. Place the tin behind the cat. This represents the cheese.

Choose another child to be the mouse. They must steal the cheese from the sleeping cat and return to their place, concealing the cheese behind their back. The cat may then uncover their eyes. They are allowed three chances to identify the mouse. If they are correct, the mouse becomes the new cat. If they don't guess who the mouse is, they remain as the cat for another game.

Comments

This game may be played with any item that makes a noise when picked up.

Vary the characters involved: try a captain and a pirate.

Not today, thank you

SEAL skill

We know how to control our behaviour and stay calm when we need to.

Resources

None

What to do

Ask the children to form a circle and choose a child to begin the game. This child must turn to the person on their right and make a funny face or do something amusing in an attempt to make the other person laugh, speak or smile. The other child must not react, other than to say 'Not today, thank you!' If they do this successfully, they turn to the person on their right and try to make them react, and so on round the circle.

Any child who reacts in any of the ways mentioned is eliminated from the game after they have attempted to make the person on their right react. The game continues until there is one child left. This child is given the title of the Great Controller because they have proved that they have excellent self-control. Their reward is to be allowed to choose the next game.

Comments

For a more difficult game, limit the ways in which a child may elicit a reaction from the child on their right.

Beat the bounce

SEAL skill

We know how to take turns and wait patiently.

Resources

A large bouncy ball

What to do

Ask the children to form a standing circle. Tell them that each member of the circle has three lives in this game. Give the ball to one child to begin the game. They bounce the ball five times in front of themselves using one hand. They then bounce it to the child on their right. The ball travels round the circle in this manner.

If a child bounces the ball an incorrect number of times or loses control of it, they lose a life. If a child loses all their lives, they sit down. When the ball has been round the circle three times, the children who still have three lives left play against each other until there is a winner.

Comments

If the group is large, you might want to use more than one ball. Alternatively, play more than one game at the same time and allow the winners to play against each other.

French cricket

SEAL skill

We can cope with frustration and disappointment.

Resources

A cricket bat or tennis racket and a small ball

What to do

Choose a child to use the bat and ask the other children to spread out round the batter as fielders. Give the ball to another child to start. They throw it at the batter, attempting to hit them below the knees. If they manage to do so, they become the new batter.

The batter is allowed to hit the ball away using the bat. If they manage this, they can move round the playing area so that they are in a good position to defend themselves against the next throw. However, if they miss the ball, they must stay where they are.

When a fielder has the ball, they must throw it from the place where they received it. If a fielder catches the ball before it bounces after the batter has hit it, they become the new batter.

Comments

Limit the amount of time a batter can be in by allowing a specific number of hits before they must swap or by setting a time limit.

Box the beanbag

SEAL skill

We can cope with frustration and disappointment.

Resources

A large box and a beanbag

What to do

Ask the children to form a circle and place the box in the centre of it. The children need to be at least ten of their paces away from the box.

Choose a child to start the game by attempting to throw the beanbag into the box. If they fail, they must retrieve the beanbag, take a step forward and try again. This continues until they are successful. They must remember the number of throws it took them to get the beanbag into the box. They then give the beanbag to the child on their right to have their go.

The child who took the lowest number of throws is the winner. If more than one child has the same low score, they can take part in a play-off.

Comments

Use more than one beanbag for a faster game, making sure that they are distributed around the circle to avoid congestion.

I had a little puppy

SEAL skill

We can abide by the rules.

Resources

A long skipping rope

What to do

Choose two children to turn the rope and a third to skip. While skipping this child says the chant below. Allocate the roles in the chant to other children. When they hear their role mentioned they have to attempt to join/leave the group skipping.

I had a little puppy and

His name was Tiny Tim.

I put him in the bathtub

To see if he could swim.

He drank up all the water. He ate up all the soap.

The next thing you know he had a bubble in his throat.

In came the doctor. (Child jumps in)

In came the nurse. (Child jumps in)

In came the lady with the alligator purse. (Child jumps in)

Out went the doctor. (Child jumps out)

Out went the nurse. (Child jumps out)

Out went the lady with the alligator purse. (Child jumps out)

Comments

Encourage the children to create their own skipping rhymes using the above structure.

Numbers

SEAL skill

We can accept that winning and losing is part of life.

Resources

None

What to do

Ask the players to form a circle and choose a child to begin the game by calling out 'One'. The child on their left then calls out 'Two', at which the child on their left calls out 'Three', and so on round the circle. Each child must remember their number.

Once all the children have said their number, establish a four-part rhythmical pattern using body sounds, such as one slap of the right knee, one slap of the left knee, one click using fingers on the right hand, one click using fingers on the left hand. Player 1 says their number and another number as sounds three and four in the pattern are made. The player with the relevant second number then says their number and another number, and the pattern continues.

If a child fails to respond when their number is called, keep the pattern going and allow them another opportunity. If they're still not successful, Player 1 calls, 'Stop, you're out!' and that child sits down. Player 1 restarts the game. A seated child may rejoin the game if their number is called along with an instruction to stand.

Comments

The rhythm may be speeded up or slowed down to make the game more or less difficult.

Going fishing

SEAL skill

We can work safely with another person.

Resources

None

What to do

Choose two children to be a net and ask them to hold hands. The other players are fish. The net must chase the fish and try to catch them. If the net is able to close their free hands round a fish safely then that fish is caught. The net must take the fish to the harbour – the side of the playground. When there are two fish in the harbour, they can form a net and return to the game. In this way, the number of nets increases. The last remaining fish is the winner.

Comments

Emphasise the need for the nets to be careful when catching fish in order to avoid any injuries.

Sharks and fishes

SEAL skill

We can be gentle even when excited.

Resources

None

What to do

Choose one child to be the shark and another to be the fish. Ask the remaining children to form a circle, holding hands with the person on either side of them and with their legs apart. Ask the shark to stand outside of the circle and the fish to stand inside it.

On your word, the shark must try to capture the fish. The children in the circle must try to block the shark's attempts to get into the circle without causing any injuries. If the fish goes outside of the circle, they are unprotected and will need to get back inside quickly.

If the shark catches the fish, the shark gets another go. If they don't catch the fish after a reasonable time, stop the game and choose a new shark and fish.

Comments

Increase the number of sharks for a quicker game.

Vary the animals used: try using a lion and a gazelle or a rabbit and an eagle.

How are you?

SEAL skill

We are gentle and respectful even when wound up.

Resources

None

What to do

Ask the children to stand in a circle and choose a child to be the leader. This child must walk round the outside of the circle and tap two children on the shoulder who are next to each other. These children step out of the circle and the child who tapped them takes one of their places.

The two children outside of the circle shake hands three times and say, 'How do you do?' They each must turn through 180 degrees and run round the circle, with the aim of being the first to get to the empty space next to the leader. When they meet round the circle, they must stop and shake hands politely three times and say, 'Very well, thank you.' They then continue the race to occupy the spare place. The winner stays in the circle and the loser becomes the new leader.

Comments

Change the wording each game to keep the children thinking.

Eggs in the nest

SEAL skill

We are gentle and respectful even during an exciting game.

Resources

Five beanbags and a piece of chalk

What to do

Draw a circle approximately 30 centimetres in diameter on the playground. Place the beanbags in this circle. Draw a circle about 1.5 metres in diameter round the smaller circle. This is the nest.

Choose a child to be the eagle. They stand inside the larger circle and must try to protect their eggs (the beanbags) from the other children. The other children must try to grab the eggs without entering the circle or touching the eagle. They may attempt to distract the eagle, but not be rude or unkind.

When all the eggs have been stolen or an agreed amount of time has elapsed, choose a new eagle.

Comments

Alternatively, when all the eggs have been stolen, the eagle must cover their eyes while the eggs are hidden. They must then attempt to find them. The child who hid the last egg to be found becomes the new eagle.

Vary the diameter of the outer circle depending on the children playing the game.

Wandering tribes

SEAL skill

We remember that other people may have very different lives from ours.

Resources

None

What to do

Divide the children into two groups of equal number. Name one group Wanderers and the other group Villagers. Ask the two groups to stand with their backs to each other.

Tell the villagers that they must decide quietly as a group if they are going to offer food, water or shelter to the wanderers. Tell the wanderers to decide independently which of these options they are going to ask for. Use the following mimes for the three options:

- Food – rub stomach
- Water – cup hands together
- Shelter – put arms above head like a pitched roof.

On your word, the wanderers must turn round and say what they each want. At the same time, the villagers must show what they are offering. Any wanderers whose request matches what the villagers are offering may join the villagers' group. When all the wanderers have been saved, make two new groups and play the game again.

Comments

Create different scenarios using the same gameplay, linking with any school projects if appropriate.

Rag tag

SEAL skill

We know how to be gentle and still have fun.

Resources

Two PE hoops and two sets of strips of material, each set a different colour

What to do

Divide the children into two teams. Give each player in a team a strip of material of the same colour, which they must partially tuck in their waistband or back pocket. Make sure that they have not tucked it in too far.

Put each hoop a suitable distance apart, and allocate one per team.

On your command, the children attempt to grab the strips of material from the other team's players. When they have a piece of the opposing team's material, they put it in their hoop. The team that gets the most pieces in a certain time, or who gets all the other team's pieces, is the winner.

Comments

Play the game with each child operating as an individual, collecting as many strips as they can in a set time.

Come up smiling

SEAL skill

We know that our moods can affect other people.

Resources

None

What to do

Ask the children to form a circle. Explain that they need to look serious and solemn. Choose one child to be Big Smiler. Tell Big Smiler that they must walk round the circle and try to make each child in turn smile back at them. If anyone smiles or laughs, they must keep their head lowered for a count of 20.

If Big Smiler decides that they want to change with someone in the circle, they may wipe the smile from their face by stroking their mouth with their hand and blowing it to another player, who becomes the new big smiler.

Comments

Big Smiler may team up with a partner and form the welcome committee. They work together to try to make the other children smile or laugh.

Changing feelings

SEAL skill

We can recognise the feelings of others by reading their body language.

Resources

None, although a list of emotions might be useful

What to do

Ask the children to form a circle and choose one child to be the leader. Ask the leader to go round the circle giving each child the name of an emotion. Each child needs to make a suitable facial expression and adopt appropriate body language for their emotion.

The leader calls out two of the emotions used and the relevant children must run into the centre of the circle. Each of these children must swap their emotion with another of the children in the centre of the circle, before running back to a different place in the circle. While this is happening, the leader has to try to occupy one of the empty spaces. If they are successful, they choose an emotion for themselves. The child left without a place becomes the new leader.

Comments

The leader may call 'All change', at which point children in the circle may change the emotion they are portraying for one of the other ones on show in the circle.

The same game

SEAL skill

We understand that diversity and similarity are important human characteristics.

Resources

None

What to do

Ask the children to form a circle with each member standing an arm's length from the child on either side of them. Ask each child in turn to share one unusual or interesting thing about themselves. If nobody in the circle feels that they share this in common with the speaker, the child who spoke remains in their place. However, if someone does feel they have this in common with the speaker, they take one step forward, as does the speaker. This continues until everyone in the circle has had two or three chances to share something, or until everyone is close to the centre of the circle.

Comments

If everyone is near the centre of the circle, ask the children to join hands together, raise them above their heads and chant 'Same, same, but different.'

Put up, put down

SEAL skill

We can be kind to others.

Resources

None

What to do

Ask the children to form a circle and choose a child to stand in the middle as the leader. Tell the children in the circle to walk slowly in a clockwise direction, so the circle rotates, chanting:

Will you do it?	*Will you do it?*
Won't you do it?	*Won't you do it?*
Will you change your mind?	*Only if it's kind.*

On the word 'kind', everyone stops moving and claps their hands once. The leader then points at a child in the circle and tells them to do something kind. The circle then counts to three. At the end of the count, the child must say, 'Yes, I'll do it.' or 'No, I won't do that. Give me another command.' If their reason for doing something is dubious, the leader has the right to ask them to explain their choice.

At any time, the leader may choose someone else to take their place in the centre of the circle.

Comments

Ask the leader to think of something that presents a moral dilemma so that the answer isn't obvious.

Birthdays

SEAL skill

We know how to be kind and generous to one another.

Resources

None

What to do

Ask the children to form a circle. Choose a child to have an imaginary birthday as part of this game. The player to their right then says what present they would give them if money were no object. The giver of the present supplies a reason for their choice of gift, such as 'I would give you a bicycle because you like to keep fit.'

When everybody in the circle has stated what present they would give, the chosen child selects the present that they would most like to receive and gives their reason. The person who thought of this present becomes the new leader.

Comments

Play a memory game in which each member of the circle has to recite the ever-lengthening list of presents before adding their present to the end.

Show some emotion

SEAL skill

We know that all people have feelings, but understand that they might show these in different ways.

Resources

A piece of chalk

What to do

Use the chalk to draw a square on the ground that is divided into four smaller squares through its centre point. Label each smaller square with the name of an emotion, such as anger, sadness, excitement and peace.

Choose a child to be the leader and ask them to stand to one side of the playing area. Ask the other children to move from one smaller square to another. At the leader's word, the children must stop where they are. They must then mime or act in a manner that reflects the emotion of the square they stopped in. The leader then gives another signal and the children move on.

Comments

Omit the chalked shape and allow the leader to call an emotion of their choice instead, which the children must then depict. The leader chooses their favourite depiction and this child becomes the new leader.

Shaping feelings

SEAL skill

We know how to read people's body language to understand what they're feeling.

Resources

None

What to do

Divide the children into pairs and ask them to form a circle with each child standing next to their partner. Each pair needs to agree which member will be Child A and which will be Child B. Ask each pair in turn to go into the centre of the circle. When in the centre, Child A chooses an emotion and moves Child B like a mannequin into a position that depicts that emotion. The other children then try to guess what emotion is being expressed. When someone guesses correctly, they move into the centre of the circle with their partner to demonstrate their emotion.

If a pair goes into the centre of the circle more than once, they swap roles in their pair.

Comments

Each pair performs a short scene that they've discussed beforehand in which the circumstances leading up to an emotion being experienced are shown. The other children have to guess what emotion the pair had chosen.

Mirror

SEAL skill

We like to practise our looking skills.

Resources

None

What to do

Ask the children to stand in a line facing you. Ask a child to come forward and turn to face the other children. This child is the performer. They need to perform a short mime, action or song to the group.

Explain that the other children are mirrors. When the performer chooses one of them, they need to perform exactly what they have just seen. Make sure all those that perform get a round of applause.

Comments

You might want to ask everyone to copy the performer's actions at the same time, instead of allowing individuals to be asked.

You know me

SEAL skill

We can listen carefully to other people.

Resources

None

What to do

Divide the children into pairs and ask them to agree which member will be Child A and which will be Child B. Ask the As to form a line facing forwards. Ask the Bs to form a line facing the As and standing opposite their partner.

Ask the As to tell their partner two pieces of information about themselves. Ask the Bs to do the same. Ask the Bs to each take one step to their right so that they are facing a new partner. The Child B at the end of the line must run to the other end of their line where there will be a Child A available. The new pairs then repeat the sharing of information. Continue in this way until each Child B is back with their original partner.

Discuss what each child can remember of what they were told.

Comments

You might want to give some categories for the information to be shared.

Cops and robbers

SEAL skill

We can try to help others when they need it.

Resources

None

What to do

Choose a child to be the robber and ask them to stand away from the group while you choose another child to be the cop. Tell the other children, including the cop, to spread out in the playing area. Tell the robber that they must chase the other children and try to tag them. Remind them to do this gently. If a child is tagged, they must stand still. If the cop touches them on the shoulder, they are able to join in the game again. If the cop is tagged by the robber, the cop is out of the game, in which case the game may continue until everyone has been tagged, or an agreed period of time has elapsed.

Comments

Play the game with two robbers, two cops or both.

Building blocks

SEAL skill

We can agree on a plan and take instructions calmly.

Resources

None

What to do

Divide the children into two groups – the audience and the builders. Tell the builders that they have a short time to agree on a scenario to portray and how they will do this. It might be a pop concert, a prize giving, a kitchen scene, playing in the park, and so on. When the time has elapsed, one of the builders stands before the audience and adopts their pose in the tableau. One by one, the other builders do the same thing. When all the builders are in place, ask the audience to guess what the scene is depicting. The groups then swap roles.

Comments

You might want to have a list of scenarios for the builders to pick from to give some guidance.

Hot potato

SEAL skill

We can identify and express a range of feelings.

Resources

A soft ball or beanbag

What to do

Ask the players to form a circle and choose a child to stand in the middle. Give the ball to someone in the circle. They must throw the ball to a child of their choosing in the circle. This child must say the name of an emotion in a way that represents that emotion before throwing the ball to another child. If they hesitate, they must swap places with the child in the centre of the circle. If the child in the centre of the circle intercepts the ball, either by catching it directly from a throw or picking it up when a child drops it, they swap places with the child who threw the ball.

Comments

Use a football that must be kicked or headed by the children. In this case, the child in the middle must gain control of the ball using their feet. Alternatively, use a large ball that must be bounced across the circle.

North, south, east and west

SEAL skill

We know that we can't always be winners and are pleased for others when they are winners.

Resources

A navigational compass and four PE markers

What to do

Ask the children to stand in the centre of the playground and choose a child to be the leader. The leader must use the compass to place the markers at the edge of the playground – due north, south, east and west.

The leader calls out one of the directions, which everyone must run to, touch the marker and return to the centre of the playground. The last child to do this is out of the game. The game continues in this way until only one child is left, who becomes the leader for the next game.

Comments

Use more than four markers for a more complex game. Add a marker for each of the following: north-east, north-west, south-east and south-west. Alternatively, allow the leader to call more than one direction in a sequence.

Colour catch

SEAL skill

We understand that things don't always go our way and can take our turn at being 'out' of games or activities.

Resources

Two balls, each a different colour

What to do

Ask the children to form a circle and choose a leader to stand in the centre of it with their eyes closed. Give the balls to different children in the circle. Ask the children to pass the balls from child to child in a clockwise direction round the circle. The leader is allowed to call any one of the following, depending on the colours of the balls:

- Red
- Blue
- Before red
- Before blue
- After red
- After blue.

When one of the above is called, the balls must be held still. The child that the statement relates to is out of the game.

Comments

You might want to play this game with more balls and instructions that are more complex.

You could play the game with two circles running at the same time, with children who are out in one circle joining the other circle.

The trickster's choice

SEAL skill

We can think quickly when under pressure.

Resources

A soft ball

What to do

Ask the children to form a circle and choose a child to be the trickster. They stand in the centre of the circle and hold the ball. On your word, the trickster may throw the ball to anyone in the circle. When they do so, they must call either 'Head' or 'Catch'. The child receiving the ball must do the opposite of what the trickster tells them. If they don't manage this, they are out. If the receiver responds correctly, they return the ball to the trickster and the game continues. The trickster needs to play quickly in order to try to catch the other children off guard.

Comments

If heading the ball is too difficult, you might want to change the instruction to 'Bounce', 'Roll', and so on.

The magic finger

SEAL skill

We can lead a group when we need to.

Resources

None

What to do

Ask the children to stand in a group and choose a leader. Explain that the leader has magic powers in this game, and so when they point a finger to the sky the other children must obey their commands. The leader may command the group to pretend to be an aeroplane, drive a car, hop like a rabbit, and so on. The group must carry out this command until a new one is given.

If the leader points at another child and says 'Now your finger is magical', this child becomes the new leader and the game continues.

Comments

Have two leaders, one at either end of the playground. The other children must move from one leader to the other in the manner commanded.

Jumbled jobs

SEAL skill

We know how to keep calm in stressful situations.

Resources

None

What to do

Ask one child to leave the group briefly while the other children choose a job and think of things that are associated with that job. If they choose hairdresser, they might include the following words: scissors, comb, mousse, gel, brush, and so on. When this has been done, ask the player who left the group to rejoin it.

At your command, the group calls out the words that they had previously chosen, although they must not say the profession. The child who left the group must try to gather the information they need in order to guess what job is being referred to.

Comments

Try the same game with other themes, such as curriculum areas, letters of the alphabet, and so on.

Fizz buzz

SEAL skill

We can concentrate even when excited.

Resources

None

What to do

Ask the children to form a circle and choose a player to start the game. They begin by saying 'One'. The child on their right says 'Two', and so on round the circle. If a number is a multiple of five, the child must say 'Fizz' instead of the number. If the number is a multiple of seven, the child must say 'Buzz' instead of the number. If a number fits both categories, the child must say 'Fizz buzz'.

Comments

Adapt the rules to other multiples, depending on the ability of the group.

Pass the invisible object

SEAL skill

We are considerate and gentle.

Resources

None

What to do

Ask the children to form a circle and choose a child to start the game.
Ask them to think of an item to be passed round the circle.
Encourage them to be creative in their choice. They must then pass
this imaginary item in a careful and considerate way to the child on
their right. The child might decide to pass a baby, a kitten, a football,
a lion or a tea tray.

The children need to watch each other to ensure that everyone treats
the item with care.

Comments

You might want to ask the children to pretend they are passing a parcel.
If someone calls 'Change', the child holding the parcel must pretend to
remove its paper wrapping carefully to reveal an object inside.

Green light, red light

SEAL skill

We are learning how to cope with disappointment when things don't go our way.

Resources

None

What to do

Choose a child to be the leader and ask them to stand at the edge of the playground with their back to the rest of the group. The other children need to move as far away from the leader as they can, while still staying within hearing distance of them.

If the leader calls 'Green light', the other children must run to them. However, the leader is allowed to turn around at any point and call 'Red light'. If this happens, the other children must stop and stand still. Any child who fails to stop promptly is out of the game. The remaining children return to their starting positions and a new round is played.

Comments

You might want to adapt the rules so that a child isn't out if caught. Instead, they may walk while the others may run.

I'm happy

SEAL skill

We know how to follow someone's actions.

Resources

None

What to do

Teach the group the following chant and actions. Choose a child to lead the group in the chant.

I'm happy, happy, happy (Clap, clap clap)

In the morning. (Mime waking up)

I'm happy, happy, happy (Clap, clap clap)

In the night. (Mime being asleep)

I'm happy, happy, happy (Clap, clap, clap)

When I eat my lunch. (Mime eating)

I'm happy, happy, happy (Clap, clap, clap)

When I write. (Mime writing)

I'm happy, happy, happy (Clap, clap, clap)

In the sunshine. (Hold arms up, high and wide)

I'm happy, happy, happy (Clap, clap, clap)

In the rain. (Wiggle fingers like raindrops)

I'm happy, happy, happy (Clap, clap, clap)

When I come to school. (Mime walking on the spot)

I'm happy to go home again. (Mime walking again)

Comments

Ask the children to come up with their own versions of this chant.

Band, book or beast

SEAL skill

We can think quickly under pressure and accept that mistakes might be made.

Resources

A soft ball

What to do

Ask the children to form a circle and choose a child to stand in the centre of it with the ball. They must throw the ball to someone in the circle, attempting to catch them off guard. At the same time, they must say 'Band', 'Book' or 'Beast'. They then begin to count to 10. If the child receiving the ball names something that fits the category before the count is completed, they change places with the child in the centre. No words are permitted that have already been used. If they fail to name something in the given time, they are out of the game and must sit down.

Comments

Try different categories to keep the game fresh and interesting.

Chinese whispers

SEAL skill

We know how to listen and respond appropriately.

Resources

None

What to do

Ask the children to form a circle and choose a child to start the game. They need to think of a simple message that they then whisper to the child on their left. This child is not allowed to ask them to repeat the message. They must whisper the message that they thought they heard to the child on their left, and so on round the circle. When the message returns to the child who devised it, they tell the group what the original message was and what the message was that reached them round the circle.

Comments

You might want to give the children time before the game to think of the message they might send, should they be asked.

Popping corn

SEAL skill

We can have fun together.

Resources

None

What to do

Ask the children to form a circle and number the children round the circle starting from one. Choose a child to be the leader and ask them to go into the centre of the circle. Tell the other children to crouch down with their feet flat on the ground and their arms round their legs. They are each pretending to be a piece of popping corn ready to pop. The leader then starts counting from one. When a child hears their number, they must jump up and continue to jump up and down. Soon all the children in the circle will be jumping and the game may begin again.

Comments

The leader may count down from the highest number in the circle, or call out the children's names for a more random sequence.

It's the way that you do it

SEAL skill

We know that feelings and behaviour are linked.

Resources

None

What to do

Choose a child and ask them to stand out of earshot of the group for a couple of minutes. Ask the other children to form a circle and to agree on an adverb, such as happily, nervously or angrily. When decided, call the child who stood to one side back to the group. This child needs to ask members of the group to mime a task in the manner of the adverb. They continue to do so until they feel confident that they know the adverb, at which point they make a guess.

Comments

You might want to limit the adverbs the group may choose until they get used to the game.

Caterpillar

SEAL skill

We can be gentle and supportive.

Resources

None

What to do

Ask the children to form a forward-facing line and then to sit down in that line. Their knees must be bent and their feet flat on the ground. Tell each child to hold the ankles of the child sitting behind them.

When ready, the line must move forward and remain intact. Calling out which foot to move for each step helps to coordinate the group's movements.

Comments

You might like to hold caterpillar races between different teams.

Fortunately, unfortunately

SEAL skill

We learn from using our speaking and listening skills.

Resources

None

What to do

Ask the children to form a circle. Choose a child to make up the first sentence of a story that must begin with the word 'fortunately'. The child on this child's right must add the next sentence of the story, which needs to begin with 'unfortunately'. This alternating pattern continues round the circle. When the story has completed a full circuit of the circle, choose a different child to start a new story.

Comments

Play the same game but try using the words 'suddenly' and 'however'.

Two little dicky-birds

SEAL skill

We can keep to rules in order to enjoy each other's company.

Resources

A long skipping rope

What to do

Choose two children to turn the skipping rope and another child to chant the rhyme while skipping.

The other children listen to the skipping rhyme below being chanted. If their name is mentioned, they need to join in the skipping.

I love coffee. I love tea.
I want (Name) to come in with me.
Two little dicky-birds sitting on a wall,
One named Peter. One named Paul.
(Both children wave)
Fly away, Peter. Fly away, Paul.
(The two children jump away from the rope)
Don't come back until your birthday is called.
January, February, … December.
(Each child rejoins when the month of their birthday is called)
Now fly away, fly away, fly away all.
(Both children jump away from the rope)

Comments

Ask the children to find out what skipping rhymes their families know and make a collection of them.

Training

Training available from Jenny Mosley Consultancies

Jenny Mosley's Whole School Quality Circle Time model is well established in thousands of schools throughout the UK and beyond. Jenny has drawn together a number of highly experienced, well-qualified consultants whose wide-ranging skills cover many areas within education.

Our courses are for all educators – encompassing head teachers, teachers, learning mentors, behaviour support teams, teaching assistants, educational psychologists, administrative support teams and many others.

For more information about training, contact
Jenny Mosley Consultancies:

Telephone: 01225 767157

Email: circletime@jennymosley.co.uk

Website: www.circle-time.co.uk

Write to: 28a Gloucester Road, Trowbridge, Wiltshire, BA14 0AA

Books and Resources

Books for playtimes

Mosley, J. (1993) *Turn your School Round.*

Mosley, J. (1996) *Quality Circle Time.*

Mosley, J. (1998) *More Quality Circle Time.*

Mosley, J. and Sonnet, H. (2002) *101 Games for Self-Esteem.*

Mosley, J. and Sonnet, H. (2002) *Making Waves.*

Mosley, J. and Sonnet, H. (2003) *101 Games for Social Skills.*

Mosley, J. and Sonnet, H. (2005) *Better Behaviour through Golden Time.*

Mosley, J. and Thorp, G. (2002) *Positive Playtimes.*

Resources for playtimes

Mosley, J. (2004) Reward Certificates.

Mosley, J. (2004) Stickers.

Mosley, J. (2004) Playground Friends Cap.

Mosley, J. (2005) Golden Rules Posters.

Mosley, J. (2005) Playground Stars.

All these resources are published by LDA. For information about the full range of Jenny Mosley's books and resources, please contact LDA Customer Services on 0845 120 4776 or visit our website at www.LDAlearning.com